WEIRD THINGS CUSTOMERS
SAY IN BOOKSTORES

WEIRD THINGS CUSTOMERS SAY IN BOOKSTORES

JEN CAMPBELL

ABRAMS IMAGE
NEW YORK

Cataloging-in-Publication Data is available from the Library of Congress

ISBN: 978-1-4683-0893-8
eISBN: 978-1-4683-1240-9

Printed and bound in the United States
5 7 9 10 8 6 4

Abrams Image books are available at special discounts when purchased in
quantity for premiums and promotions as well as fundraising or
educational use. Special editions can also be created to specification.
For details, contact specialsales@abramsbooks.com or the address below.

Abrams Image® is a registered trademark of Harry N. Abrams, Inc.

ABRAMS The Art of Books
195 Broadway, New York, NY 10007
abramsbooks.com

For bookstores and heroic booksellers everywhere
with thanks to our loyal customers, without whom
we wouldn't be selling books

And to all the people within these pages who've kept
me on my toes, made me smile and scared the
absolute *hell* out of me—thank *you*

CONTENTS

INTRODUCTION

I grew up in the northeast of England (on a diet of books and biscuits) and, when I went to Edinburgh University to study literature, I decided to get a part-time job. It made sense to get a job in a bookstore, considering that's where I spent most of my time in the first place. So, in 2008, I started work at the Edinburgh Bookshop, a wonderful independent bookstore in the Scottish capital, owned by Vanessa and Malcolm Robertson. They have a dog called Teaga, a huge Leonberger, who served as a mascot for the store. We'd tell children she was the dog from Peter Pan. They believed it, and they loved it. I loved it, too.

I'd only been working in bookselling about a month when I realized that some customers really do say the craziest, rudest, and absolute weirdest things imaginable. As I was standing by the register one Saturday, a lady came up and said she'd just finished reading *The Diary of Anne Frank*. She had really liked it, and she wondered if Anne had ever written a sequel. I nearly choked on my tea! At first I thought she was joking, but the look on her face told me she was quite serious. This was the first "weird thing" a customer said to me but, as you'll see, it was far from the last.

When I graduated, I moved down to London where I now work in a rare bookstore called Ripping Yarns. It's been around since the 1930s, but when the new owner, Celia, took the shop over in the 1980s, Terry Jones and Michael Palin (of Monty Python fame) were on hand for the grand reopening, hence the store's new name. The venue changed but the weird things continued; in fact, they increased! There's just something about old books and the odd requests they create.

After a particularly strange day about a year ago in which I was asked if books were edible, I started putting some choice "Weird Things Customers Say..." quotes up on my blog (jen-campbell.blogspot.com). The intent wasn't to mock or antagonize our customers. Far from it. Most of the people I meet everyday are amazing, an integral part of our north London neighborhood and the lifeblood of our business in a tough time for booksellers. But, as anyone who works in retail probably knows, there are some encounters that simply leave you speechless.

Very quickly, links to the quotes I posted were thrown around Twitter by other bookstores and book-lovers who found them amusing. Neil Gaiman liked the posts and blogged about them, opening them up to an even wider audience. (Thank you, Neil!) After that, a publishing company in the UK got in touch and asked if I'd like to think about making "Weird Things..." into a book, and here we are! A full-length collection, illustrated by the fantastic Brothers McLeod.

The response from the book community has been spectacular thus far, and for this American edition, we've rallied booksellers all over and asked them to send in quotes of their own experiences. So, in these pages, if the quotes aren't credited, they are mine and, if they are, then they've been submitted by fellow booksellers across the United States and Canada. It was extremely reassuring to know that customers are saying bizarre things all over the place. Long live bookstores—and all our customers!

Sometimes bookselling is the best job in the world, and sometimes it isn't (as you'll soon find out). However, one thing is for sure: it's definitely never boring!

—JEN CAMPBELL, 2012

LITERARY PURSUITS

Customer: Where are your copies of *Breaking Dawn*? I can't see any on the shelf.

Bookseller: Sorry, I think we've sold out of the *Twilight* books; we're waiting on more.

Customer: What?

Bookseller: We should have some more in tomorrow.

Customer: But I need a copy now—I just finished the third one last night.

Bookseller: I'm sorry, I can't help you.

Customer: No, you don't understand, I've taken the whole day off work to read it.

Bookseller: Erm...

Customer: I NEED TO KNOW WHAT HAPPENS! NOW!

Bookseller: Erm...

Customer: Can you call your wholesaler and see if they can deliver this afternoon?

Bookseller: They only—

Customer: And then I can wait here for the book to arrive.

Bookseller: I'm sorry, they only deliver in the mornings.

Customer: BUT WHAT AM I SUPPOSED TO DO NOW?

Bookseller: ... We have many other books.

Customer *(sniffs)*: Do any of those have Robert Pattinson in them?

◆

Customer: Do you have any crime books about speeding tickets?

◆

Customer: Did Charles Dickens ever write anything fun?

◆

GOOD TIMES

by

CHARLES DICKENS

Bookseller: Can I help you find anything?

Customer: Yes. Where are your books with *words*?

Lanora Haradon
Next Chapter Bookshop, Mequon, WI

Customer: I want to buy a book for my mother. She likes Danielle Steel.

Bookseller: Here she is, under "S" for Steel.

Customer: ...Well, I don't know which ones she's already read... Do you?

Bookseller: ...

Eve Taggart
Half-Price Books, Atlanta, GA

Customer: Where's your true fiction section?

Betsy Urbik
Barnes and Noble, Rockford, IL

Customer: This *Abraham Lincoln: Vampire Hunter* book has to be the most historically accurate fiction book I've read.

Carrie Austin
Island Bookstore, Kitty Hawk, NC

Customer: I'm looking for a biography to read that's really interesting. Could you recommend one?

Bookseller: Sure. What books have you read and liked?

Customer: Well, I really loved *Mein Kampf*.

Bookseller: ...

Customer: Loved is probably not the right word.

Bookseller: No. Probably not.

Customer: Liked, is probably better. Yes. Liked. I liked it a lot.

Bookseller: ...

Customer: Do you have a book of mother-in-law jokes? I want to give it to my mother-in-law as a joke. But, you know, not really as a joke at all.

Customer: Do you have a copy of *Atonement*? But not the film cover, please. Keira Knightley's neck makes me want to punch things.

Customer: Do you have any books containing passages which would be suitable to read out at a funeral?

Bookseller: Sure, I'll help you look.

Customer: Thanks.

Bookseller: And I'm sorry for your loss.

Customer: Oh, don't worry about it; it's just my daughter's guinea pig.

Customer: If I had a bookstore, I'd make the mystery section really hard to find.

Anonymous

Customer: Can you help me find a book, please?

Bookseller: Sure, what are you in the mood for?

Customer *(leaning in very closely)*: I'm feeling very
  vulnerable right now.

Meaghan Beasley
Island Bookstore, Kitty Hawk, NC

Customer: Where's your poetry section?

Bookseller: It's just over here.

Customer: Great. Do you know who wrote the poem "Happy Birthday to you, you live in a zoo, you look like a monkey, and you smell like one too"?

Bookseller: ...

Customer: Do they have their own collection?

Customer: Do you have a copy of *Jane Eyre*?

Bookseller: Actually, I just sold that this morning, sorry!

Customer: Oh. Have you read it?

Bookseller: Yes, it's one of my favorite books.

Customer: Oh great *(sits down beside bookseller)*. Could you tell me all about it? I have to write a paper on it by tomorrow.

Bookseller: Can I help you at all?

Customer: No, I don't think you're qualified. I need a psychiatrist—that's the only help I need.

Bookseller: .... Ok.

Rachele Willey
Waterstone's East Grinstead, UK

◆

Customer: Hi, could you recommend a book for me?

Bookseller: Sure. What kind of thing are you looking for?

Customer: Well, I was let out of jail this morning, so something not too heavy would be nice.

◆

Customer: Wow, you have a lot of neat stuff here. I wish I read.

Customer's friend: Yeah, if it's not in *People Magazine*, I don't care.

Gabe Konrád
Bay Leaf Used & Rare Books, Sand Lake, MI

◆

(Customer arrives at desk with two baby books, a stuffed bunny toy, and Lolita *by Vladimir Nabokov)*

Bookseller: That's an interesting selection you've got there.

Customer: They're all for different people.

Jason Rosenberg
National Bookstore Chain, Winnipeg, MB

◆

Customer: Do you have a book on the Enlightenment?

Bookseller: Sure.

Customer: Excellent. My son's just about to start studying it at school. It's all about the light bulb being invented, right?

Customer: Hi, I've got a book on reserve and I've come to pick it up.

Bookseller: Sure, what's your name, and what was the title of the book?

Customer: My name's Stuart and it was volume one of *The Waverley Children's Dictionary*.

Bookseller: I'm sorry, I can't see that on our reserve shelf. When did you come in and reserve it?

Customer: Oh, it was a while ago now.

Bookseller: A couple of weeks?

Customer: No... more like a year and a half.

Bookseller: I'm afraid we only reserve books for a month and then they have to go back out in the store. We don't have the space to keep them to one side for longer.

Customer: But I was really looking forward to reading that!

◆

Customer: Do you have any of those books where you can change the names of the main character to the name of the person you're giving the book to? Do you have *Alice in Wonderland*, but not Alice; I'd like *Sarah in Wonderland*.

Bookseller: I'm afraid you have to buy those from the publisher, as they're a print on demand service.

Customer: Yeah, I don't really have time to do that. Do you have a copy of *Alice in Wonderland*? Then I can just cross out the name myself and change it.

Customer: Where do you keep *Hamlet*? You know "to be or not to be"? Is it in with philosophy?

Customer: I wonder if they have a book putter-backer; someone who puts back the books. I could do that and be paid in books.

David Enyeart
Common Good Books, St. Paul, MN

Customer: Who wrote *Winnie the Pooh*?
Bookseller: A. A. Milne.
Customer: Ah, yes, that's right. She hasn't brought out anything new in a while, has she?
Bookseller: He. And no, you're right, he hasn't.

Customer: Do you have any Robin Hood stories
where he doesn't steal from the rich? My
husband's called Robin and I'd like to buy him
a copy for his birthday, but he's a banker, so ...

WHAT WAS THAT TITLE AGAIN?

♦

(A couple approaches the desk)

Bookseller: Can I help you find something?

Man: Yeah, we're looking for a vocabulary book. It's either called *The Soars* or *The Sars*.

Bookseller: Let me look it up and see what we have.

Woman: Oh, it's ok, I made a note of the title.

(Customer pulls a napkin from her purse and lays it down for the bookseller to read. Written on it is: "The Saurus.")

Anonymous

♦

Customer: Do you have a copy of *Nineteen Eighty Six*?

Bookseller: *Nineteen Eighty Six*?

Customer: Yeah, Orwell.

Bookseller: Oh—*Nineteen Eighty Four*.

Customer: No, I'm sure it's *Nineteen Eighty Six*; I've always remembered it because it's the year I was born.

Bookseller: ...

◆

Customer: My granddaughter's looking for a book about Agnes's knickers... do you know what I mean?

Bookseller: Agnes's knickers... Ah! Louise Rennison can be found over here.

(Bookseller hands customer a copy of Angus, Thongs and Full-Frontal Snogging*)*

◆

(At a university bookstore)

Customer: I'm looking for a book for my Northern Anthropology Class.

Bookseller: I'm afraid I'm not familiar with that class. Do you know the title, or have your syllabus with you?

Customer: No.

Bookseller: Right. What's your overall course in?

Customer: Literature.

Bookseller: Oh. *(pause)* So, not anthropology?

Customer: No.

Bookseller: Right. Are you looking for the *Norton Anthology*?

Customer: Yes, that's it!

Megan McCluskey
College Bookstore, NJ

◆

Customer: Do you have *Campbell's Soup for the Soul?*

Glen Robbe
Books Inc, Mountain View, CA

◆

Customer: I'm looking for some books on my kid's summer reading list. Do you have *Tequila Mockingbird*?

Anonymous

◆

Customer: Do you have the CliffNotes for *The Poems of Jimmy Stewart*?

Anonymous

◆

Customer: Do you have Agatha Christie's *Death in Denial*?

◆

Customer: May I have a copy of *The Tiger's Wife*? How did she live with Tiger Woods all those years!

Mary Jane Reed
G. J. Ford Bookshop, St. Simons, GA

Customer: I don't know why she wants it, but my wife asked for a copy of *The Dinosaur Cookbook*.

Bookseller: *The Dinah Shore Cookbook*?

Customer: That must be it; I wondered what she was up to.

Elizabeth Durand
Bookland of Maine, ME

Customer: There was a book in the eighties that I loved... but I can't remember the title.

Bookseller: Can you remember anything about it?

Customer: I think it was called *360 Fairy Tales*.

Bookseller *(searches on a central catalogue)*: Nothing under that name, sorry.

Customer: I might have got the number wrong. Could you just type in "fairy tales" and see what comes up?

Bookseller: That could take a while.

Customer: Do you have that Enid Blyton series? Not *The Secret Seven*—the other one.

Bookseller: *The Five Find Outers*? *The Famous Five*?

Customer: Yes, *The Famous Five*, that's the one. The one with the transsexual.

◆

Customer: Excuse me, but do you have *Flowers for Arugula*?

Pam Price
Book Shop of Beverly Farms, Beverly Farms, MA

Customer: Hi, my kid needs *The Count of Monte Crisco* for Honors English.

Betsy Weitzman
Borders, King of Prussia, PA.

Customer: I'm looking for *Canary Row*.

Jason Frost
Russo's Books, Bakersfield, CA

Customer: Do you have any Willa Catheter?

Anonymous

Customer: Do you have *Fiddler on a Hot Tin Roof*?

Jan Weissmiller
Prairie Lights Books, Iowa City, IA

Customer: I need *A Few Good Men* by Joe Steinbeck.

Bookseller: Do you mean *Of Mice and Men* by John Steinbeck?

Customer: No, I said *A Few Good Men*.

Bookseller: The movie?

Customer: No. It's a classic book! Steinbeck.

Bookseller: I don't see that here by him. But he did write *Of Mice and Men*.

Customer: What? Just show me where to find his books.

(Later)

Customer: Here it is. *Of Mice and Men*. Right there on your shelf.

Jade Hollingsworth
Vroman's Bookstore, Pasadena, CA

PARENTS AND KIDS

Customer: My kids are just climbing your book-shelves. That's ok, isn't it? They won't topple over, will they?

Customer: It makes me sad that grown-up books don't have pictures in them. You're brought up with them when you're younger, and then suddenly they're all taken away!

Bookseller: Yes. It's a cruel world.

Customer: These books are really stupid, aren't they?

Bookseller: Which ones?

Customer: You know, the ones where animals, such as cats and mice, are best friends.

Bookseller: I suppose they're not very realistic, but then that's fiction.

Customer: They're more than unrealistic; they're really stupid.

Bookseller: Well, writers use that kind of thing to teach kids about accepting people different to themselves, you know?

Customer: Yeah, well, books shouldn't pretend that different people get on like that, and that everything is "la de da" and wonderful, should they? Kids should learn that life's a bitch, and the sooner the better.

Customer: I do find it odd that people manage to make a living out of writing books for kids. I'm sure any mother could do it.

Bookseller: Why don't you try it yourself?

Customer: I always mean to, but I'm very busy right now with my pottery class.

Customer: I'm looking for a book for my son. He's one of these weird people who still likes the paper ones.

Anonymous

Customer: Do you have a book with a list of careers? I want to give my daughter some inspiration.

Bookseller: Ah, is she applying for college courses?

Customer: Oh no, not yet. She's just over there. Sweetheart?
(a four-year-old girl comes over)

Customer: There you are. Now, you talk to the nice lady, and I'm going to find you a book on how to become a doctor or a scientist. What do you think about that?
(the girl says nothing)

Customer *(to bookseller)*: Won't be a sec.
  (Customer wanders off into non-fiction)
Bookseller: So, what's your name?
Child: Sarah.
Bookseller: Sarah? That's a beautiful name.
Child: Thank you.
Bookseller: So, Sarah, what do you want to be when
  you grow up?
Child: … A bumblebee.
Bookseller: Excellent.

◆

(Customer comes into the store with her five-year-old son)

Customer: Come on, Jason, take your shoes off.

Bookseller: It's ok... you don't have to take your shoes off to come into the bookstore.

Customer: Please don't encourage him. I'm trying to train him to remember to take his shoes off in the house because we've got new carpets. The more he does it, the more he'll remember.

◆

Customer: I'm looking for a book for my son. He's six.

Bookseller: How about this one. It's about—

Customer: Yeah, whatever, I'll take it.

◆

Customer: I'm just going to run to the store to do the weekly food shopping. I'm just going to leave my sons here, is that ok? They're three and five. They're no trouble.

◆

Child: Mommy, can we buy this book?

Mother: Put that down, Benjamin. We've got enough books at home!

◆

(A child is playing with a book on the floor and rips it)

Child's mother: Oh, Stephen *(she tuts in a non-serious way)*. Do be careful. *(She takes the book off the child and puts it back on the shelf)*

Bookseller: Excuse me?

Child's mother: Yes?

Bookseller: Your son just ripped the head off the tiger who came to tea.

Child's mother: I know. Children, eh?

Bookseller: Yes, but we can't sell that book now. It's damaged.

Child's mother: Well I don't know what you expect me to do about it.

◆

(Child finds the light switch and begins to flick it on and off... and on and off)

Child's mother: He's playing a game he calls Night and Day.

Bookseller: Could you please ask him to stop? I need to be able to see the register to help these customers.

Child's mother: It's ok. He'll stop in a few minutes. See, he's pretending to snore at the moment. He'll stop soon and pretend to wake up, and switch the light on like it's the sun. He's so imaginative, isn't he? David, what time is it in the game?

Child: It's five in the morning!

Child's mother *(to bookseller)*: See. Not long to go now. Just be patient.

◆

Child: Mom, how did Anne Frank escape the Nazis?

Mother: I'll tell you later.

Child *(screaming)*: BUT I WANT TO KNOW NOOOOOOWWW!

Bookseller *(to fellow bookseller):* Someone should tell her she kept away from the Nazis for so long by being quiet.

Anonymous

◆

Customer: If my daughter wants to buy books from the teenage section do you need to see some form of ID? It was her thirteenth birthday this weekend. I can show you pictures of the cake. You can count the candles.

◆

Child: Mom, look, it's the book of *101 Dalmatians*. Can I get a hundred and one puppies?

Child's mother: No, you've already got a hamster. That's quite enough.

◆

Customer: Do you have any positions available at the moment? I'd like my daughter to get a Saturday job.

Bookseller: If your daughter is interested in working for us, it'd be best if she came and spoke to us herself.

Customer: I don't think she's that keen on having a job, that's the problem... But you could always come round to our house and try and convince her to come and work for you. Then she might consider it.

◆

Customer: I'm looking for a book for my son. He's only seven but he's so advanced; it's like he has the brain of a twenty-year-old. What would you recommend?

◆

Customer: Hi, my daughter is going to come by on her way home from school to buy a book. However, she seems to like to buy books with sex in them, and she's only twelve, so can I ask you to keep an eye out for her and make sure she doesn't buy anything inappropriate for her age? I can give you a list of authors she is allowed to buy.

Bookseller: With all due respect, would it not be easier for you to come in with your daughter?

Customer: Certainly not. She's a grown girl; she can do it herself.

Customer: Ok, so you want this book?
Their daughter: Yes!
Customer: Peter Pan?
Their daughter: Yes, please. Because he can fly.
Customer: Yes, he can—he's very good at flying.
Their daughter: Why can't I fly, daddy?
Customer: Because of evolution, sweetheart.

Customer: Did Beatrix Potter ever write a book about dinosaurs?

Customer *(to their friend)*: God, the *Famous Five* titles really were crap, weren't they? *Five Go Camping. Five Go Off in a Caravan....* If it was *Five Go Down to a Crack House* it might be a bit more exciting.

Parent: *(to a misbehaving child)*: THERE SHOULD BE NO YELLING UNLESS SOMEONE IS ON FIRE!

Child: *(firing back immediately)*: What about if a weasel is robbing the store?

Parent *(long pause… with the flickering of a smile)*: I don't know… is he armed?

Richard Due & Elizabeth Prouty
Second Look Books, Prince Frederick, MD

Customer: Oh, look, they've got a section on dictionaries. Perhaps we should get your brother one for school, for Spanish, what do you think?

Her daughter: Can we get one for when we go to Scotland for our holidays?

Customer: They speak English in Scotland, too, sweetie.

Five-year-old girl: Mommy, I could stay in here all day!

Mother: I don't know why you read; it'll never get you anywhere.

Christopher Sheedy
Re: Reading, Toronto, ON

YOU WANT WHAT?

Customer: I read a book in the sixties. I don't remember the author, or the title. But it was green, and it made me laugh. Do you know which one I mean?

Customer: This might be a stupid question, but do you sell milk?

Customer: Do you sell lottery tickets?

Customer: Do you have any sea-monkey food?

James Crossley
Island Books, Mercer Island, WA

Customer: Do you sell swimming goggles?
Bookseller: No, I'm afraid we do not.
Customer: And you call yourself a full service book-
store?
Bookseller: ...

Emily Crowe
Odyssey Bookshop, South Hadley, MA

Customer: Do you sell bed sheets?

Kathleen Elder
Borders Express, Tucker, GA

Customer: Do you sell screwdrivers?

Customer: Do you sell gum?
Bookseller: No, we're a bookstore. We sell books.
Customer: Oh. Right. *(pause)* What about cigarettes?
Bookseller: Nope, still just a bookstore.

Anonymous

Customer: Didn't this place used to be a camera store?

Bookseller: Yes, it did, but we bought the place a year ago.

Customer: And now you're a...

Bookseller: ... a bookstore.

Customer: Right. Yes. So, where do you keep the cameras?

◆

Man: Where are the pianos?

Bookseller *(leading him towards the music section)*: Sheet music is on the bottom shelf; piano tuning and repair books are on the next shelf up.

Man: No, no, no! I need a piano.

Bookseller: We don't sell pianos.

Man: I hear music.

Bookseller: ...That's the radio.

Man: Are you sure?

Ann Salisbury
Bienville Books, Mobile, AL

◆

Customer: Hi, I just wanted to ask: did Anne Frank ever write a sequel?

Bookseller: ...

Customer: I really enjoyed her first book.

Bookseller: Her diary?

Customer: Yes, the diary.

Bookseller: Her diary wasn't fictional.

Customer: Really?

Bookseller: Yes... She really dies at the end— that's why the diary finishes. She was taken to a concentration camp.

Customer: Oh... that's terrible.

Bookseller: Yes, it was awful.

Customer: I mean, it's such a shame, you know? She was such a good writer.

Customer: Do you have any books in this shade of green, to match the wrapping paper I've bought?

Customer: Do you arrange your books by color? I'm looking for a blue book.

Emily Crowe
Odyssey Bookshop, South Hadley, MA

Customer: You know how they say that if you gave a thousand monkeys typewriters, then they'd eventually churn out really good writing?

Bookseller: ... Yes.

Customer: Well, do you have any books by those monkeys?

Bookseller: ...

◆

Customer: How about dragons? Do you have any books with dragons?

Bookseller: Well, let me check. There are tons of books with dragons in them; I can pull up a list if you like.

Customer: Can you get any with pictures of real dragons?

Mike Tennyson
Bay Brooks, Great Mills, MD

◆

Customer: Do you have a copy of *Bridget Jones: The Edge of Reason*? I can't see it on the shelf.

Bookseller: I'm afraid we don't, but I can order it for you, and it'll be here in the next forty-eight hours. We could even mail it to you if you like?

Customer: I don't trust the postal service. Could you fax it instead?

◆

Customer: Do have that book about those people in that place with the thing?

Anonymous

Customer: Do you have any medical textbooks?

Bookseller: Sorry, no. They go out of date so quickly that we don't stock them, but I can order one for you.

Customer: I'm not worried about it being in date.

Bookseller: Does your course not request you have a specific edition?

Customer: Oh, I'm not a medical student, I just want to learn how to do stitches.

Bookseller: ... Right.

Customer: Do you have a book on sewing, instead?

Customer: Do you have any books signed by Margaret Atwood?

Bookseller: We have many Margaret Atwood books, but I'm afraid we don't have any signed by Margaret Atwood, no.

Customer: I'm looking for a birthday present for my wife. I know she'd really love a signed copy. You couldn't fake a signature could you?

Customer: Do you have any books by Jane Eyre?

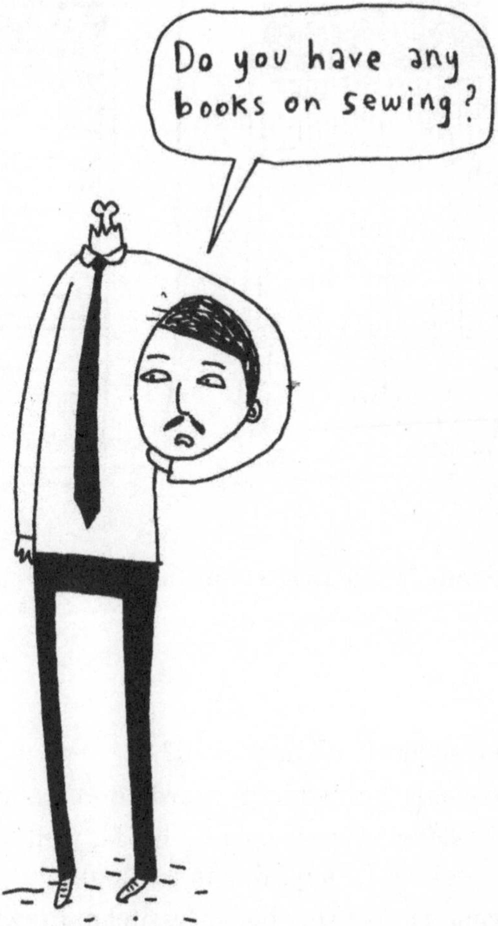
Do you have any books on sewing?

Customer: Where are your fictional novels?

Bookseller: Can I help at all?

Customer: Yes, where's your fiction section?

Bookseller: It starts over on the far wall. Are you looking for anything in particular?

Customer: Yes, any books by Stefan Browning.

Bookseller: I'm not familiar with him, what kind of books has he written?

Customer: I don't know if he's written any. You see, my name's Stefan Browning, and I always like to go into bookstores to see if anyone with my name has written a book.

Bookseller: ... Right.

Customer: Because then I can buy it, you see, and carry it around with me and tell everyone that I've had a novel published. Then everyone will think I'm really cool, don't you think?

Bookseller: ...

Customer: Do you have a crafts book on how to build a gun?

Bookseller *(on the phone)*: Hello, Ripping Yarns
  Bookstore.

Customer: Hi. Do you have any mohair wool?

Bookseller: Sorry, we're not a yarns store, we're a
  bookstore.

Customer: You're called Ripping Yarns.

Bookseller: Yes, that's "yarns" as in stories.

Customer: Well it's a stupid name.

Bookseller: It's a Monty Python reference.

Customer: So, you don't sell wool?

Bookseller: No.

Customer: Hmph. That's ridiculous.

Bookseller: ... But we do sell dead parrots.

Customer: What?

Bookseller: Parrots. Dead. Extinct. Expired. Would
  you like one?

Customer: Erm, no.

Bookseller: Ok, well, if you change your mind, do
  call back.

Customer: I'd like to buy your heaviest book, please.

◆

Customer: Do you have this book *(holds up a biography)* but without the photographs?
Bookseller: I think the photographs are published alongside the text in every edition.
Customer: Why?

Bookseller: I suppose it's so you can see what everyone looked like.

Customer: I don't like photographs.

Bookseller: Ok.

Customer: Could you cut them out for me?

Bookseller: ...

◆

Customer: Hi there.

Bookseller: Hi, can I help?

Customer: Yes, I was just admiring your store sign outside.

Bookseller: Thank you.

Customer: It's really lovely...

Bookseller: ...Yes.

Customer: ... Is it for sale?

◆

Customer: If I came to work here, would I get a discount at the liquor store next door?

◆

(Phone rings)

Bookseller: Hello?

Person: Hi there, can I speak to the manager of the property?

Bookseller: Speaking. How can I help?

Person: I'm calling to see if you'd be interested in stocking some cleaning products in your vicinity.

Bookseller: To sell?

Person: Yes.

Bookseller: We're a bookstore.

Person: Yes. Could you see yourselves branching out into this area?

Bookseller: Not really, no.

Person: How about I send over a sample of products and you can see how you get on?

Bookseller: No, thank you.

Person: Books and cleaning products work well together.

Bookseller: Do they?

Person: I'm sure we could make this work.

Bookseller: No, thank you.

Person: I think you're missing out on a very interesting opportunity. Can you think of any other bookstores that might be interested?

Customer: Do you have a book on how to breathe underwater?

Bookseller: You mean Julie Orringer's short story collection: *How to Breathe Underwater*?

Customer: Is that fact?

Bookseller: No, it's fiction—the title's a metaphor.

Customer: ... Oh. No. I need a book on how to actually breathe underwater.

Bookseller: ...

Customer: Do you have a book on dinosaurs? My grandson's really into them.

Bookseller: Absolutely, we have one over here.

Customer: Does it have every type in it?

Bookseller: I believe it's a very comprehensive collection, yes.

Customer: Great. So, does it have a chapter on dragons?

◆

Customer: Do you have any old Elvis CDs?

Bookseller: No, we don't sell music, sorry. We might have a book on Elvis, though.

Customer: Would any of those come with a life size cut out of him?

Bookseller: ...I doubt it.

◆

Customer: Do you have *Dr. Who and the Secrets of the Hidden Planet of Time*?

Bookseller: I'm not familiar with that one. Hang on and I'll check our system for you.

Customer: Thank you.

Bookseller: I'm afraid I can't find it on our database, or a reference to it online. Are you sure you've got the right title?

Customer: No, not at all. I don't know that it actually exists.

Bookseller: ... What do you mean?

Customer: Oh, I was just driving to work yesterday and I thought up the title and I thought "now that sounds like the kind of book I'd like to read," you know?

Bookseller: Hmmm. Well, I'm afraid you can't read it, as it hasn't been written.

Customer: Never mind, never mind—just thought I'd check.

Bookseller: We do have lots of other Dr. Who novels over here, though, if you'd like to take a look.

Customer: No, it's ok. I'll go home and have another think and come back again.

Customer: Hi, my best friend came in last weekend and bought a book, and she really loved it. Do you have another copy?

Bookseller: What was the title?

Customer: Oh, right. Yeah. I don't remember.

Customer: I'm looking for that famous book—you know, the Disney one, where Donald Duck is an accountant.

◆

Customer: Do you have an easy version of "Moonlight Sonata" for piano?

Bookseller: We have a box of sheet music by the music books section. I'll have a look.

Customer: Thanks.

Bookseller: Yep. Here's a "Moonlight Sonata" for grade two.

Customer: And that's easy?

Bookseller: Compared to the real thing, yes.

Customer: So, I should be able to play it, yeah?

Bookseller: I don't know. How long have you been playing?

Customer: Oh, I don't know how to play, I thought I'd just try.

Bookseller: Right. Can you read sheet music?

Customer: Well... sure... it's just the alphabet, isn't it?

◆

Customer: I'm looking for a book about this big *(indicates size)*. I've got a space on my bookshelf and I need to fill it. It's really bugging me.

Bookseller: What kind of book would you like?

Customer: I don't care, just as long as it's exactly this size.

◆

Customer: Where do you keep your maps?

Bookseller: Over here, what kind of map are you looking for? A county, a state, a world map?

Customer: I want a map of the sun.

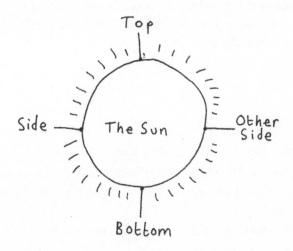

Customer: Is your poetry section split up into rhyming and non-rhyming sections?

Bookseller: No, it's just in alphabetical order. What kind of poetry are you looking for?

Customer: Rhyming. Preferably iambic pentameter, of poems of no more than ten lines, by a female poet. But, other than that, I don't mind.

Customer: Hi, do you sell Christmas trees?

Bookseller: No...

Customer: Oh. I thought it was worth asking because you've got lots of Christmas books in the window.

(Phone rings)

Bookseller: Hello, Ripping Yarns bookstore.

Customer: Hi. My friend recommended you to me. She said you sell the most amazing knee high socks.

Bookseller: We don't sell socks, we're a bookstore.

Customer: Oh, have you sold out?

Bookseller: Of what?
Customer: Of socks.
Bookseller: No, we're a *book*store.
Customer: Oh, ok.

◆

Customer: I'd love to hold a fashion photo shoot in here. We could get models to come in and half bury themselves in books on the floor, or get them to hang from the bookshelves. Do you think your customers would mind?

Customer: I've been looking through your geography section—I can't find any books on Atlantis.
Bookseller: You know, I think we managed to lose those.

Customer *(holding up a book about knitting)*: Do you think I could knit using my own hair?

Customer: What books could I buy to make guests look at my bookshelf and think: "Wow, that guy's intelligent"?

Customer *(on the phone)*: Do you have *(inaudible)*?
Bookseller: I'm sorry?
Customer: Do you have miso soup?
Bookseller: Um, no... this is a bookstore.
Customer: But it says Book S... Oh. Never mind.

Amelia Cone
Book Soup, West Hollywood, CA

Customer: Do you have any books on Japan?

Bookseller: Sure. A travel guide or a history?

Customer: Yes.

Bookseller: Which one?

Customer: Both.

Bookseller: Right.

Customer: ... And it should also have stories for children.

Bookseller: ...

Customer: Illustrated.

Bookseller: ...

Customer: And it has to be a hardback, not a paperback. And it should be a good price.

Bookseller: ...

Customer: A really nice old edition, with a modern twist.

Bookseller: ... I'm really not sure what kind of book you're looking for.

CUSTOMERS BEHAVING BADLY

CUSTOMERS BEHAVIOUR GROUP

Customer *(holding up a copy of a Harry Potter book)*: This doesn't have anything weird in it... does it?

Bookseller: You mean, like, werewolves?

Customer: No *(whispers)* —gays.

Bookseller: ... Right.

◆

(Local author comes into bookstore, lifts his books from the bookshelf and starts rearranging them on the table in the middle of the room)

Bookseller: What are you doing?

Local Author: Well, they're never going to sell just sitting on a shelf, are they?

◆

Customer: Which was the first Harry Potter book?

Bookseller: *The Sorcerer's Stone.*

Customer: And the second?

Bookseller: *The Chamber of Secrets.*

Customer: I'll take *The Chamber of Secrets*. I don't want *The Sorcerer's Stone.*

Bookseller: Have you already read that one?

Customer: No, but with series of books I always find they take a while to really get going. I don't want to waste my time with the useless introductory stuff.

Bookseller: The story in Harry Potter actually starts right away. Personally, I recommend that you start with the first book—and it's very good.

Customer: Are you working on commission?

Bookseller: No.

Customer: Right. How many books are there in total?

Bookseller: Seven.

Customer: Exactly. I'm not going to waste my money on the first book when there are so many others to buy. I'll take the second one.

Bookseller: ... If you're sure.

(One week later, the customer returns)

Bookseller: Hi, did you want to buy a copy of *The Prisoner of Azkaban*?

Customer: What's that?

Bookseller: It's the book after *The Chamber of Secrets*.

Customer: Oh, no, definitely not. I found that book far too confusing. How on earth are children supposed to understand it if I can't? I mean, who the heck is that Voldemort guy anyway? No. I'm not going to bother with the rest.

Bookseller: ...

◆

Customer: Do you have an LGBT fiction section?

Bookseller: We don't have a specific section, but we do have LGBT literature—Sarah Waters, Ali Smith, Jeanette Winterson, Christopher Isherwood etc. Which author were you looking for?

Customer: Don't worry, I'll have a look through the fiction section—thanks for your help.

Other Customer: Sorry, did I hear you right? Did you just say that all the homosexual books are in with the normal fiction.

Bookseller: All our fiction is one section.

(Other Customer looks suspiciously at the book she's holding and slides it back on the shelf)

◆

Customer: I'm looking for a book for my eleven-year-old daughter. What would you recommend? I'd like something educational, too, not anything nonsensical.

Bookseller: Well, how about something like *When Hitler Stole Pink Rabbit*? She'll be doing the Second World War at school soon, and this is about Judith Kerr's life. She had to travel across Europe when she was a little girl because her father was a German journalist outspoken against Hitler, and it's about her joining schools in France and England, and learning new languages.

Customer: I don't really want her to learn about all that Hitler Nazi nonsense. It's all so long ago, now, and completely irrelevant. It's tedious.

(Customer is reading a book from the shelf, pauses and folds the top of one of the pages over, then puts it back on the shelf)

Bookseller: Excuse me, what are you doing?

Customer: I was just reading the first chapter of this book, but I'm going to be late meeting a friend for lunch. So, I'm just marking it and I'll finish reading it when I stop by tomorrow.

(Customer walks around the store, eating peanuts and throwing the shells on the floor.)
Bookseller: Sir, we don't allow food in the store.
Man: This isn't food! It's a snack!

Ann Salisbury
Bienville Books, Mobile, AL

Customer *(shouting from the doorway)*: Do you have any jobs going at the moment? I'd come in and talk properly, but I'm really busy.

Customer: I'd like a refund on this book please.

Bookseller: What seems to be the problem?

Customer: I barely touched it. It's ridiculous!

Bookseller: What do you mean?

Customer: I mean all I did was drop it in the bath by accident. And now, I mean, just look at it: the thing's unreadable!

(Phone rings)

Customer: Hi, I'm looking for any books by Kenneth Roberts.

Bookseller: One second, and I'll have a look for you.
(Bookseller checks the shelves)

Bookseller: I'm afraid we don't have any right now.

Customer: What? You mean you're all out of BOOKS?

Lisa Morton
Iliad Bookshop, North Hollywood, CA

Customer *(speaking loudly into her phone)*: Why aren't you here yet? I don't like walking around with two thousand in cash on me! Hurry up and pick me up!

Customer: Can I return this book? I'm allergic to ink.

Dale Szczeblowski
Porter Square Books, Cambridge, MA

(Phone rings)

Bookseller: Hello?

Customer: Hi there. I have a complaint I'd like to make.

Bookseller: I'm sorry to hear that; what seems to be the problem?

Customer: My daughter's been having nightmares about *The Gruffalo*.

Bookseller: Right.

Customer: What are you going to do about it?

Bookseller: Well, I hasten to add that I have never heard of a child having nightmares about *The Gruffalo* before. It's certainly not meant to be a scary book, and I'm sure the person who recommended this book to you didn't intend for this to happen either. When did you buy this book from us?

Customer: We didn't buy it from you.

Bookseller: ... Right.

Customer: I'm calling from Canada. I've googled all the bookstores I can find, and I'm calling you up to request that you stop stocking the book immediately.

Bookseller: ... Right.

(Pause)

Customer: So, are you going to get rid of the copies that you do have?

Bookseller: No, I'm afraid we won't be doing that.

Customer: And why is that?

Bookseller: Because this appears to be an isolated incident, and the book is loved by many of our customers.

Customer: Right... I see. Well. I'll be splitting my daughter's counseling bill and sharing it among heartless booksellers like you!

Bookseller: Out of interest, how many bookstores have agreed to get rid of the book so far?

Customer: I think you'll find that that's beside the point.

(Phone goes dead)

◆

Customer *(holding up a Jamie Oliver cookbook)*: Would you mind if I photocopied this recipe?

Bookseller: Yes, I would.

◆

Customer: Have you read...

Bookseller: ...

Customer: Oh, nevermind. You look too young to have read a good book.

> *Madison Butler*
> *Liberty Bay Books, Poulsbo, WA*

Bookseller: Ok, so with postage costs that brings your total to $13.05. One second and I'll get the card machine.

Customer: No. No, absolutely not. I demand that you charge me $12.99. I will not pay for anything that starts with thirteen. You're trying to give me bad luck. Now, change it, or I will find a bookstore that doesn't want me to fall down a hole and die. Ok?

Customer: Hi, I've just self-published my art book. My friends tell me that I'm set to be the new Van Gogh. How many copies of my book would you like to pre-order?

Bookseller: You know, Van Gogh was never appreciated in his lifetime.

Customer: ...

Customer *(poking his head round the door)*: Hi, can I bring my dog inside?

Bookseller: Sure, there's a sign on the door that says that friendly dogs are allowed.

Customer: Well, she's not that friendly; she might bite people.

Bookseller: ... Well then please leave her outside.

◆

Customer: I don't suppose I could have a cup of coffee, could I?

Bookseller: Well... erm....

Customer: Thanks, I'd really like one.

Bookseller *(indicating the bookshelves)*: Have you seen anything you'd like?

Customer: Oh, I'm not buying. I'm just waiting for my bus.

Customer: You only have the hardback of this book.

Bookseller: Yes. It's only available in hardback, I'm afraid.

Customer: Oh, but, can't you call the publisher and insist that I want the paperback? Can't they just print it on demand for me?

Samantha Beiko
Type Books, Toronto, ON

Customer *(peering over)*: Do you have brown eyes?

Bookseller: Yes, I do.

Customer: My mother told me never to trust anyone with brown eyes.

Bookseller: ... You have brown eyes.

Customer: ...

(Phone rings)

Bookseller: Thanks for calling Barnes and Noble, how can I help you?

Customer: Yeah, hi, um... do you sell Scrabble dictionaries?

Bookseller: Yes, of course. Do you want me to put one on hold for you?

Customer: Oh, no that's okay. But, listen, I'm about to win this round, can you check to see if "Kennedy" is included?

Anonymous

◆

Customer: My dear, there's a long line at the post office, and I only want a stamp for this letter. Do you have one I could buy from you?

Bookseller: No, I'm sorry, I don't.

Customer: Well then, perhaps you could go and stand in the line for me? You're a lot younger than me; your legs can handle it.

Bookseller: I'm afraid not—I'm running this bookstore by myself, so I can't leave.

Customer: I'll keep an eye on it for you.

Bookseller: No, I'm sorry, I'm afraid I can't do that; I'd get in a lot of trouble.

Customer: Well. You've been extremely unhelpful. *(she storms out)*

Dear Sirs,

I am writing to see if you have any positions available at your bookstore. I really love your store, and the personalized service I get from you when I've been in previously. Your store is one dear to my heart.

I have attached my résumé.

Best,

(someone who CC'd this email to every bookstore in the city)

(Man enters bookstore smoking a cigarette)

Bookseller: Excuse me?

Man: Yes?

Bookseller: Could you put that cigarette out, please?

Man: Why?

Bookseller: Because it's illegal to smoke in a public place.

Man: This isn't a public place; there's only you and me here.

Bookseller: Yes, well, it's still a public place. And, apart from anything else, this store is rather flammable.

Man: Why?

Bookseller: ... because it's filled with paper.

Man: Is it?

◆

Customer *(via email)*: Please, I would like to know if this book has any mildew smell. If not, I will order it as soon as possible. I have one copy but I don't like the smell. Thank you.

Customer: I called earlier about *Slaughterhouse Five* for my class?

Bookseller: Yes. I have a copy here for you.

Customer: Okay, thanks. What's your return policy?

Bookseller: ... Why?

Customer: Because I only need it for, like, a week.

Lillian Clark
The Second Story, Laramie, WY

Customer *(poking her head round the door, glancing at our 18 x 18 foot bookstore)*: Do you have a café in here?

Bookseller: No, I'm afraid we don't.

Customer: Oh, I was looking for a bookstore with a café.

Bookseller: If you want a cup of tea, there's a café four doors down.

Customer: Could I take some books there with me to look through and browse? And then bring them back?

◆

(A man walks around the store, carrying a plastic bag stuffed with Nike jackets)

Man *(to a customer)*: Would you like to buy a Nike jacket?

Customer: Erm, no.

Man: *(to another customer)*: Can I interest you in a Nike jacket? Genuine Nike.

Bookseller: Excuse me, what are you doing?

Man: I was just seeing if anyone would like to buy a jacket.

Bookseller: Please don't bother my customers.

Man: But it's a store … they're here to buy things.

◆

Customer: Do you do gift wrap?

Bookseller: No, I'm afraid we don't, sorry.

Customer: I tell you what; I'll run to the store across the road and buy some wrapping paper. Then I'll bring it back and you can wrap the book up for me, ok? You're a bookstore, for Christ's sake, you're here to offer me a service.

◆

Customer: Wow, you have a whole bookcase of Enid Blyton books?

Bookseller: Yep, we do. *Famous Five, Secret Seven, Five Find Outers, Noddy*—all of it there.

Customer: I loved the *Famous Five* when I was younger.

Bookseller: Yes, they were fun.

Customer: I'm so glad you think so. I know that there are a lot of people who say that Anne, from *The Famous Five*, was stupid and that she shouldn't have just been doing the "girly" things, and that it was offensive.

Bookseller: Well...

Customer: I think all this political correctness has just gone way too far. I mean, who cares that Enid Blyton openly said that a woman should be the one to do the cooking and the cleaning? So she should.

Bookseller: Well—

Customer: —and then there are those who complain about the *Noddy* picture books, you know?

Bookseller: Hmmm.

Customer: Well, I say that a bit of racism never hurt anyone.

Bookseller: ...

Customer: Everything in moderation, don't you agree?

Bookseller: Your book will arrive in a few days. What's your phone number?

Customer: Oh, er, I can't remember it.

Bookseller: Ok. How would you like us to contact you when your book gets here?

Customer: Could you send me a postcard?

Bookseller: ...What's your address?

Customer: Oh. I'm not sure. Is it important?

Julia Sheng
Pegasus Books, Berkeley and Oakland, CA

(Customer brings The Lord of the Rings *trilogy to the counter)*

Customer: I am Legolas and I need to spread the word about *The Lord of The Rings*. I need to have this book for free.

Bookseller: No, I'm sorry, I can't give you the book for free.

Customer's friend: You have failed your quest!

Christopher Miya
Pegasus Books, Berkeley and Oakland, CA

Customer: What's your name?

Bookseller: Jen.

Customer: Hmmm. I don't like that name. Is it ok if I call you something else?

◆

Customer (*holding up a magazine from the Sixties*): It says on the front cover that this magazine was supposed to come with half a jigsaw puzzle, but you don't have the jigsaw puzzle. Does that mean I can have the magazine for free?

◆

Customer: Do you have security cameras in here?

Bookseller: Yes.

Customer: Oh. *(Customer slides a book out from inside his jacket and places it back on the shelf)*

Bookseller: Hi, can I help you?

Customer: I don't give a damn about books—they bore me.

Bookseller: I'm not sure you're in the right place, then.

Customer: No, I am. I just wanted to ask what specific color you painted your bookshelves. I love this color. I mean, the right color can make books look more appealing, can't it?

Bookseller: Can it?

Customer: And the smell of the paint takes away the smell of the books, too. Which is also a plus.

Customer: I've got a while before my bus. Are you and any of the other customers interested in playing cards?

Customer: Hi. I'm looking for a stuffed animal.

Bookseller: I'm afraid we don't really have any of those. We do have some books for babies, though. They're over here.

Customer: Er, it's for a B-A-B-Y. What's wrong with you? Babies can't read!

Anonymous

Customer: Have you read every single book in here?

Bookseller: No, I can't say I have.

Customer: Well you're not very good at your job, are you?

Man *(bursting through the bookstore door)*: Hey! Could you keep it down? We're trying to film something outside.

Bookseller: ... I'm not making any noise.

Man: Well, it looked like you were about to.

Bookseller: ... It's just me and the books here; we're not going to have a raucous party.

Man: Yeah, well... just make sure you don't.

Customer: I've forgotten my glasses, could you read the beginning of this book to me to see if I like it?

◆

Customer: You must get so much time to read, just sitting here surrounded by books.

Bookseller: What is it you do?

Customer: Me? I work in a clothes store.

Bookseller: Well, you must get so much time to try clothes on, just standing there, surrounded by clothes.

◆

(On putting the key in the door of the bookstore to open up in the morning, a customer comes up)

Bookseller: Excuse me, sorry, I'm afraid I'm not open yet. If you could wait two seconds and I'll get the boxes out of the way and put the lights on.

Customer: Oh, don't worry, I'll only be a second. *(Barges past into bookstore)*

◆

(Bookseller puts the book the customer has bought into a paper bag)

Customer: Don't you have a plastic bag? I'm sick of all this recycling nonsense. It's not doing any of us any good.

(Phone rings)

Bookseller: Hello, Ripping Yarns bookstore.

Customer: Hi there. If I buy a book and pay for it over the phone, could you bring it over the road to my house? I just live round the corner.

Bookseller: Are you unable to leave your house?

Customer: Well, no... but it's raining.

Customer: You don't have a very good selection of books.

Bookseller: We've got over ten thousand books.

Customer: Well, you don't have the book I've written! *(storms out)*

Customer: Do you have the time?

Bookseller: Yes. It's just after four o'clock.

Customer: No, it isn't.

Customer: Who do I speak to about me selling you some books?

Bookseller: That would be me.

Customer: Where's your boss? Is he not here?

Bookseller: The owner of the store isn't here, she's at home.

Customer: And who's her boss? What's his name?

Bookseller: She is the boss.

Customer: Oh. Well, you're all modern, aren't you?

(Customer is scraping his shoe along one of the display tables)

Bookseller: Sir, please don't do that; you're making the table dirty.

Customer: But where else do you expect me to scrape this gum off my shoe?

Anonymous

Customer: Do you have any jobs available?

Bookseller: Have you worked in a bookstore before?

Customer: No.

Bookseller: I take it you enjoy reading?

Customer: No, I don't read at all.

Bookseller: So... why do you want to work here?

Customer: Well, I don't really. It's just that I've moved into an apartment up the street, and I'd like a job within walking distance.

(Customer is doing push-ups in the middle of the bookstore. Lying beside him is an exercise book)

Bookseller: Excuse me, sir, what are you doing?

Customer: I don't see why I can't practice the exercises first, before buying the book!

Anonymous

Customer: I've got a lot of books that I want to look through, so I've ordered a pizza to eat while I do that. Should I have them deliver it straight to the second floor, or should I meet them at the front desk?

Anonymous

Customer: Can I just take this book to the restaurant next door and read it while I'm eating my lunch?

Barbara Pope
The Mulberry Bush Book Store, Parksville, BC

◆

Man: Do you have a restroom?
Bookseller: No, I'm afraid we don't.
Man: Well, then, I'm peeing right here. *(He does so)*

Anonymous

Customer: Is your mother around?
Bookseller: ... I run this bookstore.
Customer: Oh. Sorry.

(Customer's phone rings)
Other Customer: Will you turn that off? There
    are laws about cell phones in bookstores,
    you know!

Customer: You know, I'm not sure I've ever really
    read a whole book before...

Customer: Do you have Harry Potter book seven,
    part two?
Bookseller: Book seven is just one volume.
Customer: But the movie has two parts, so there
    must be a second book. They don't just make
    movies from nothing!

Gabe Konrád
Bay Leaf Used & Rare Books, Sand Lake, MI

Customer: We've got so many books at home that we've had to start recycling them.

Bookseller: You mean you're taking them to thrift store?

Customer: No, I mean we've actually started recycling them. You know, putting them out with the trash.

Bookseller: …

(Customer walks in and leaves the door wide open)

Other customer: Could you close that door behind you?

Customer: I'm just paying for this book, and then I'm leaving again. I'll only be two seconds.

Other customer: You've already been in here ten seconds and now it's freezing in here.

Customer: That's because you're blocking my way to the register!

Other Customer: Just close the bloody door. Where are your manners? This is a bookstore!

Customer: You wouldn't believe this woman. She reads like a bird!

Llalan Fowler
Main Street Books, Mansfield, OH

(Woman throws a piece of paper down on the desk)

Woman: I need these books.

Bookseller: I'm sorry, I can't make out this handwriting.

Woman: I can't read it either, my daughter wrote it. Just search for it.

Bookseller: I can't search for it if I don't know what it is.

Woman: Just guess!

Bookseller: Ma'am, the only word I can make out on here is "bitch."

Anonymous

ISN'T IT OBVIOUS?

Customer: Hi, I'd like to return this book, please.

Bookseller: Do you have the receipt?

Customer: Here.

Bookseller: Erm, you bought this book at Borders.

Customer: Yes.

Bookseller: ... I'm afraid we're not Borders.

Customer: But you're a bookstore.

Bookseller: Yes, but we're not Borders.

Customer: You're all part of the same chain.

Bookseller: No, sorry, we're an independent bookstore.

Customer: ....

Bookseller: Put it this way, you wouldn't buy clothes at Urban Outfitters and take them back to Gap, would you?

Customer: Well, no, because they're different stores.

Bookseller: Exactly.

Customer: ... I'd like to speak to your manager.

Customer *(to her friend)*: What's this literary criticism section? Is it for books that complain about other books?

Customer: Are all of your books for sale, or just some of them?

(*A couple enter and start to browse new hardcover fiction titles. The man picks up Philip Roth's* The Plot Against America)

Man: I've been looking for this.

Woman: What's that, honey?

Man: It's this book about what would happen if Charles Lindbergh had become president instead of FDR.

Woman: Oh. Who won that election, again? I can't remember.

Man: Uh.... Roosevelt.

Woman: Really?

Meaghan Beasley
Island Bookstore, Corolla, NC

Customer: You know that film, *Coraline*?

Bookseller: Yes, indeed.

Customer: My daughter loves it. Are they going to make it into a book?

Customer: Is this book edible?

Bookseller: ... No.

Customer: Do you run story time for children?

Bookseller: Yes, we do. It's on a Tuesday, for toddlers.

Customer: Great, the day care up the road is so expensive, and I've been dying to have a few hours to go shopping, and maybe get my nails done.

Bookseller: I'm sorry, but I'm afraid you have to
   supervise your child at story time.
Customer: Why?
Bookseller: … because we're not a day care center.

Customer: Doesn't it bother you, being surrounded by
   books all day? I think I'd be paranoid they were
   all going to jump off the shelves and kill me.
Bookseller: …

Customer: Could I bring my entire antique watch collection in to show you?

Marilyn Brooks
Battenkill Books, Cambridge, NY

Customer: Where is your section on bat books— to build a bat house?

Barbara Pope
The Mulberry Bush Book Store, Parksville, BC

Customer: Can you mail books to the jail?

Bookseller: Sure

Customer: Do you have a list of all your true crime books?

Cathy Allard
BayShore Books, Oconto, WI

Customer: Will you be open so I can buy the new Harry Potter book?

Bookseller: Yep, we're having a midnight opening.

Customer: Great. What time?

Customer: I've always thought I'd like to open up my own bookstore.

Bookseller: Oh, really?

Customer: Yes, definitely. There's just something about it, you know? I just think it must be ever so relaxing.

Customer: Who is the author of the Shakespeare plays?

Sheryl Cotleur
Book Passage, Corte Madera, CA

Customer: Excuse me, do you have any signed copies of Shakespeare plays?

Bookseller: Er... do you mean signed by the people who performed the play?

Customer: No, I mean signed by William Shakespeare.

Bookseller: ...

Person: Hi, I'm looking for a Mr. Patrick.

Bookseller: No one of that name works here, sorry.

Person: But does he live here?

Bookseller: ... No one lives here; we're a bookstore.
Person: Are you sure?

◆

Customer: Hi, if I buy a book, read it, and bring it
 back, can I exchange it for another book?
Bookseller: No... because then we wouldn't make
 any money.
Customer: Oh.

◆

Pizza Delivery Man (*on entering the store with a
 large pile of pizzas and seeing the bookseller,
 the only person in the bookstore*): Hi, did you
 order fifteen pizzas?

(One bright Saturday afternoon)

Customer *(walks up to counter)*: Are you open on Saturdays?

Christopher Sheedy
Re: Reading, Toronto, ON

(Phone rings)

Bookseller: Hello, Ripping Yarns Bookstore.

Man: Hello, is that Ripping Yarns?

Bookseller: Yes, it is.

Man: The bookstore?

Bookseller: ... Yes.

Man: Are you there?

Bookseller: How do you mean?

Man: I mean, are you at the store now?

Bookseller: Erm... yes, you just rang the number for the bookstore and I answered your call.

Customer: Do you sell iPod chargers?

Bookseller: ... No.

Customer: Why?

Man: Hi, I was wondering if I could ask you about a book I'm writing.

Bookseller: Sure.

Man: Well, it's here. *(He produces "book"—a series of things stuck into a pad of paper)*

Bookseller: Right, what's the premise?

Man: It's a children's book. See, I've been taking pictures of stuff and my friend has been writing poems to go alongside it.

Bookseller: Ok. Are you a professional photographer?

Man: No, I've just been taking photos of things on my cell phone. They're pretty good though, yeah?

Bookseller: Erm, well they're a little blurry.

Man: Oh, that just makes them unique.

Customer: And your friend, has he had poems published elsewhere?

Man: Nope, he doesn't believe in that kind of stuff.

Bookseller: Ok... so, what's your next step?

Man: To get it published.

Bookseller: What's your plan of action?

Man: Just send it off to publishers.

Bookseller: Which one?

Man: Any old one. All of them. It ain't hard, is it?

Bookseller: With all due respect, it is rather hard.

Man: Well our friends think it's a fantastic idea.

And I don't think it can be hard—there are books everywhere these days—just look at this store!

Bookseller: Well, yes, but we are a *book*store.

Customer: So, you sell children's books?

Bookseller: That's why it's called The Children's Bookstore.

Customer: Oh, I thought maybe it was someone's last name.

Emma Casale
The Children's Bookstore, Baltimore, MD

Customer: You have maps?

Bookseller: Yes, we do. Road maps?

Customer: Yes.

Bookseller: We have old ones, and new ones, over here.

Customer: I need map to the south coast.

Bookseller *(has a look)*: I'm not sure we have a specific southeast map. We have a road map, though, which has a map of the southeast in it.

Customer: No. I walk.

Bookseller: You're walking?

Customer: Yes.

Bookseller: To the coast?
Customer: Yes.
Bookseller: That's very very far.
Customer: It's five miles, yes?
Bookseller: No. It's about eighty miles.
Customer: You point me in the right direction?
Bookseller: I don't know which way it is from here.
Customer: Ok. I follow the smell of the sea.

◆

Customer: Did I leave my bicycle in here?

◆

Man *(looking at a giant map on the wall of the store)*: When did they move New Zealand way down by Australia? Wasn't it in Europe before?
Bookseller: ...

Christopher Sheedy
Re: Reading, Toronto, ON

◆

Customer *(on noticing Nicola Morgan's "Write to be Published" advertisement in front of the desk)*: A book on how to get published?

Bookseller: Yes. Nicola's fabulous.

Customer: Is it about self-publishing?

Bookseller: Nicola focuses mainly on mainstream publishing.

Customer: Oh, I've written that kind of book myself.

Bookseller: Have you?

Customer: Yeah. I self-published it. It isn't selling as well as I thought it would.

Customer: Oh wow, this bookstore is lovely!

Bookseller: Thank you.

Customer: I was in a bakery just like it the other day.

Bookseller: ...

(Phone rings)

Bookseller: Hello?

Customer: Are you ok?

Bookseller: Excuse me?

Customer: Is the bookstore ok?

Bookseller: Yes... the bookstore's fine, thank you.

Customer: Really? I heard that something terrible had happened.

Bookseller: ... As far as I'm aware, we're all fine.

Customer: Oh. Well, I got home from work to find a note from my daughter saying that there'd been a series of unfortunate events in the bookstore, and that I should call you about it.

Bookseller: Oh! No. You ordered Lemony Snicket's *A Series of Unfortunate Events*. You can come and pick it up whenever you're free.

Customer: ... Oh! Well, thank goodness for that.

Pam Price
Book Shop of Beverly Farms, Beverly Farms, MA

◆

Customer: Do you bother to arrange your books at all, or are they just plonked places?

Bookseller: They're in alphabetical order...

Customer: Oh.

◆

Customer: If I give you these three paperbacks, will you sell them and give the money to charity?

Bookseller: We're not a charity bookstore.

Customer: Oh. Where does your money go to?

Bookseller: ... It goes towards keeping us in business.

Customer: Someone should have taught that Shakespeare guy how to spell. I mean, am I right, or am I right?

Customer: Do you have any piano sheet music, but for guitars?

Bookseller: You mean, do I have sheet music for guitars?

Customer: Yes.

Customer: Oh, sorry. I thought you were the post office.... You're not, are you?

Customer: Do you sell dictionaries?

Bookseller: Sure. What kind of dictionary are you looking for?

Customer: One with all the words.

Charles Miller
Quiet Man Bookshop, Cresco, PA

Customer *(to her friend, upon opening a copy of* The Lord of the Rings*)*: Oh, look, this one's got a map in the front.

Customer's friend: Oh yeah. Where's it of?

Customer: Mor... Mor-dor.

Customer friend: Oh. Where's that then?

Customer: Hi, I just wanted to check: are you a bookstore, or are you a library?

Bookseller: ... We're a bookstore.

Customer: You should probably have a sign saying that somewhere; it's confusing.

Bookseller: We have a big sign outside that says "Ripping Yarns Bookstore."

Customer: Yes, well, that's ambivalent, isn't it?

Bookseller: It is?

Customer: It's amazing, isn't it, how little we really know about writers' lives? Especially the old ones.

Bookseller: I guess the lives of writers have changed a lot.

Customer: Yes. And don't forget about those women who used to write under male names.

Bookseller: Yes, like George Eliot.

Customer: I always thought Charles Dickens was probably a woman.

Bookseller: ... I'm pretty sure Charles Dickens was a man.

Customer: But who's to say?

Bookseller: Well, he was pretty prominent in society; lots of people saw him.

Customer: But maybe that was all a show—maybe that was her brother, while Charlene was at home, writing.

Bookseller: ...

◆

Customer: You should consider arranging your books by size and color.

Bookseller: But then no one would be able to find anything.

Customer: Well, that doesn't matter. It'd look pretty.

◆

Customer *(on the phone)*: Can you tell me how to get to your bookstore?

Bookseller: Sure—where are you coming from?

Customer: My house.

Deena O'Daniel
Barnes & Noble Sunset Valley, Austin, TX

◆

Customer: You know, if you put boxes of books outside you'd attract a lot more customers.
Bookseller: ... it's snowing outside right now.

◆

Customer: Can books conduct electricity?

BOOKS FOR KINDLING

(Phone rings)

Bookseller: Hello?

Customer: Hi. I was wondering if you could help me. I'm looking for a book for my niece. She's six and I've no idea what to buy her.

Bookseller: Sure. What kinds of things is she into?

Customer: I don't really know. I don't see her very often—my sister lives abroad.

Bookseller: Ok, what's her name?

Customer: Sophie.

Bookseller: Ah, well, have you considered the Dick King Smith *Sophie* series? There's even a book called *Sophie's Six*.

Customer: Ok, sure, that sounds like a good idea.

Bookseller: Do you want me to double check that we have those in stock? I'm pretty sure we do.

Customer: No, it's ok. I'm just going to order them online.

Bookseller: But... we just gave you the recommendation.

Customer: I know, and I appreciate it. It's such a pain Amazon doesn't have a function for that. But I know I can rely on you guys for advice.

Bookseller: ...

Customer: I'm from out of town. Can I recharge my Kindle here?

Tom Campbell
The Regulator Bookshop, Durham, NC

Customer: Do you sell any books with instructions for how to use my Kindle?

Carolyn Hutton
A Great Good Place for Books, Oakland, CA

Customer *(while walking up to the counter)*: Wow! I didn't realize books were still so popular!

Bookseller: ...

Anonymous

Customer: I just don't like my Kindle. I like *real* books. They are like cozy blankets to me.

Mary Jane Reed
G. J. Ford Bookshop, St. Simons, GA

Customer: Hello, I'd like a copy of *The Water Babies*, with nice illustrations. But I don't want to pay a lot of money for it, so could you show me what editions you have so I can look at them, and then I can go and find one online?

Bookseller: Can I help you find something?

Customer: No, I have an e-reader. I'm just here to get ideas and see what's new.

Anonymous

Customer: So where do all these books come from? Do you get them from Amazon?

Leslie Hawkins
Spellbound Children's Bookshop, Asheville, NC

Customer *(inclining her head)*: How are you guys doing?

Bookseller: Oh, we're clinging on.

Customer: Oh you poor dears, it's this Kindle!

Bookseller: Well, really, it's the supermarkets making people think that books aren't worth paying money for.

Customer: I hadn't thought of it like that. It is terrible, isn't it?

(five minutes later)

Customer: How much is this book?

Bookseller: That's $10.

Customer: Could I have it for $5?

FIGHT! FIGHT! FIGHT!

Customer: Do you guys sell used e-books?

Bookseller *(laughing):* No...

Customer *(angrily)*: Why not?

Kat Bailey
Bookshop Santa Cruz, Santa Cruz, CA

◆

Customer: Can I return an e-book I bought from another bookstore to you?

Kate Weiss-Duncan
Penguin Bookshop, Sewickley, PA

◆

Customer: Hi.

Bookseller: Hi there, how can I help?

Customer: Could you please explain Kindle to me.

Bookseller: Sure. It's an e-reader, which means you download books and read them on a small hand-held computer.

Customer: Oh, ok, I see. So ... this Kindle. Are the books on that paperback or hardback?

THE ADULT SECTION

Fifteen-year-old boy: Do you have a book that will
help me hook up with slutty girls?

Anonymous

Customer: Do you stock Nigella Lawson under
"sex" or "cooking"?
Bookseller: It's a tough call, isn't it?

Customer: Do you have a restricted section?

Customer: Do you keep the pornography in the
photography section?

Customer: Do you have any pop-up books on sex education?

Elderly Gentleman: Hello, do you have any books on sex?

Bookseller: I think we have a couple, yes.

Elderly Gentleman: Excellent. I've had a hip replacement, and I wasn't sure how long I had to wait, you see.

Bookseller: ... Right.

Elderly Gentleman: I bet you could look it up on that computer there, though, couldn't you?

Bookseller: ... I suppose I could, if I needed to.

Elderly Gentleman: Excellent thing, the internet.

◆

(*Picks up a biography of actress Helen Mirren*)

Customer: Jesus! Helen Mirren has *huge* boobs!

Housing Works Used Bookstore, New York, NY

◆

Customer: Hi, do you have that sperm cookbook?

Bookseller: No.

Customer: That's a shame; I really wanted to try it. Have you tried it?

Bookseller: I have not.

◆

Customer: Do you have a book that lists aphrodisiacs? I've got a date on Friday.

◆

Customer: Do you have a nature section? I'm
    looking for a nature guide, you know, for places
    to go.

Bookseller: Sure, our nature section is just down
    here.

Customer: No, sorry, not nature—naturist.

Bookseller: Oh!

Customer: Do you have any comics where the women have really big breasts? It's... er... it's for an art project.

Customer: Do you have a, er... a back room?

Bookseller: You mean a store room?

Customer: Ah, a store room. Ok. Yes.

Bookseller: Yes, we have a store room..

Customer: I'd like to *(wink)* buy something *(wink)* from your store room.

Bookseller: Excuse me?

Customer: Oh, right, you've got a buzz word, haven't you? A password?

Bookseller: I think you're mistaken. I think you're thinking of somewhere else.

Customer: Oh. Really?

Bookseller: Yes. I think you should leave now.

Customer: Oh. *(moves away)*
(Customer comes back two minutes later)

Customer: Just to clarify: I was asking for drugs and you were saying you're not that kind of place, right?

Bookseller: That's right.

Customer: Ok, thanks.

Pause

Customer: Could you recommend—

Bookseller: No.

Customer: Ok, ok… Thanks.

Bookseller: You're welcome.

Customer: Bye, then.

Bookseller: Goodbye.

Customer: Very nice bookstore.

Bookseller: Thank you.

◆

Customer: I need a two-minute contemporary monologue that like takes place in a courtroom and is about like dying from venereal disease.

Bookseller: Well, that does not exist. But you can commission me to write it.

Customer: No, it needs to be contemporary.

Theresa Buchheister
Drama Book Shop, New York, NY

◆

(Customer buying the Fifty Shades of Grey *trilogy)*

Customer: Do you sell batteries?

Gina Martindelcampo
Sparta Books, Sparta, NJ

◆

Daughter: Dad, will you buy me that book?
Dad: Which book?
Daughter: *Fifty Shades of Grey.*
Dad: No!
Daughter: Please?
Dad: No!
Mom: I have it, I'll lend it to you.
Dad *(in the tone of one deeply betrayed)*: Why do you have it?
Mom *(calmly)*: It was for the neighborhood book club.
Daughter: Nevermind.

Anonymous

HIGHER POWERS

Customer: Do you have any books on star signs?

Bookseller: Yes, our esoteric section is over here.

Customer: Good, thanks. It's just I really need to check mine—I have this overwhelming feeling that something bad is going to happen.

◆

Customer: Do you have any books on the dark arts?

Bookseller: ... No.

Customer: Do you have any idea where I could find some?

Bookseller: Why don't you try Knockturn Alley?

Customer: Where's that?

Bookseller: Oh, the center of London.

Customer: Thanks, I'll keep my eyes peeled for it.

Customer: Do you have any books on the story of Easter?

Bookseller: I'm sure we do, yes.

Customer: Excellent. Something with lots of baby roosters and rabbits would be great, thanks.

◆

Customer: Do you have any books on flying?

Bookseller: Sure, the aviation section is right over here.

Customer: No, man, I can already levitate; I need to know how to fly.

Bookseller: You can levitate?

Customer: I'm doing it right now. My shoes are hollow, so it looks like I'm standing on the ground.

Anonymous

◆

(Customer ordered a nineteenth-century book, claimed it was in terrible condition, which it wasn't, sent the book back in only a paper bag, with pieces of paper stuck to the pages that showed photographs. The spine was broken, as though he'd put said book on a photocopier, copied the images he'd marked and posted the book back to to the bookstore—never intending to keep it in the first place. The booksellers reported this to ABE.

ABE books gave the booksellers the money to repair the book, and refunded the buyer with a strong warning.)

Several very rude emails ensued with choice phrases such as:

Customer: You will not forget this transaction. Every time an event goes wrong in your life, you will remember karma... I am a prophet and I bring you this message in the name of Jesus Christ.

A few weeks later, the customer posted a letter-size envelope to the bookstore stuffed with pamphlets on how to recognize the devil within themselves.

Customer: Do you have a religious section?

Bookseller: Sure, it's just over here.

Customer: You've got Richard Dawkins's books here, next to copies of the Bible.

Bookseller: That section is for all kinds of books relating to religion.

Customer: I hope you know that's a sin. And you will go to hell.

Customer *(holding a copy of Stephen King's* Carrie*):* Does this guy write horror books?

Bookseller: Yes.

Customer: Well, I need you to move it to a different section.

Bookseller: Sorry—was it misshelved?

Customer: No, it was in horror, but I need it to go to a different area. My pastor says we should never read horror novels.

Bookseller: … oh.

(Bookseller moves the book. Customer buys it.)

Ann Salisbury
Bienville Books, Mobile, AL

(Man approaches bookseller and attempts to start a conversation with her about religion)

Bookseller: I'm sorry, sir, but I try to make a point of not discussing religion with customers.

Customer: Oh. I just thought you seemed like a nice girl, and I don't want you to go to Hell.

Bookseller: …

Lillian Clark
The Second Story, Laramie, WY

Customer: Who wrote the Bible? I can't remember.
Customer's friend: Jesus.

Customer: I saw *The Passion of the Christ* this weekend and somebody told me there was a book about it. Do you have it?
Bookseller: You mean a book the movie was based on?
Customer: Yes. I didn't see it on any of your displays.
Bookseller: Sir, the movie was based on the Bible.
Customer: The Bible?

Bookseller: Yes, sir.

Customer: Oh, the Bible! But isn't there a book?

Cassandra Chan
Borders, Jensen Beach, FL

Bookseller: Can I help you find anything?

Woman: Yes. We're looking for the portal.

Bookseller: Sorry?

Man: We're looking for the portal.

Bookseller: ….

Woman: We've been tracking the portal to Lemuria for a long time and we're pretty sure it's here.

Bookseller: In this bookstore?

Man: Yes, we've been tracking the energy for years and we're certain it's in a bookstore in Lincoln City. We're pretty sure it's this one, but it's possible it could be in a bookstore a few miles away.

Woman: No. Everything indicates it should be here. Maybe under the stairs.

Bookseller: Right. Well, have a look around, I suppose. Let me know if I can help you find anything!

Diana Portwood
Bob's Beach Books, Lincoln City, OR

Customer: Do you have a book with a photograph of Jesus in it? I want to prove to my friend that he was white.

Michael G. Martin
Barnes and Noble, Pittsburgh, PA

Customer: Do you have a book that interprets life?
Bookseller: I'm not sure I know what you mean.
Customer: Well, I was out hiking the other day, and I saw a wolf. I want to know what that meant.

Jody Mosley
Barnes and Noble, Boulder, CO

(*Punching the second to last hole on the customer rewards card*)
Bookseller: Oh look, you're getting very close to your reward!
Elderly Customer: In more ways than one!

Mary Jane Reed
G. J. Ford Bookshop, St. Simons, GA

Customer: Which way is it to the cemetery?
(*Bookseller hands over a map*)
Customer: Thanks. And that vampire that used to live there... he's dead now, right?

Customer: I'm always on night shift at work.

Bookseller *(jokingly)*: Is that why you're buying so many vampire novels?

Customer *(seriously)*: You can never be too prepared.

Lauretta Nagel
Constellation Books, Reisterstown, MD

OUT OF PRINT

Customer: What kind of bookstore is this?
Bookseller: We're an antiquarian bookstore.
Customer: Oh, so you sell books about fish.

Customer: Do you have black-and-white film posters?

Bookseller: Yes, we do. They're over here.

Customer: Do you have any posters of Adolf Hitler?

Bookseller: Pardon?

Customer: Adolf Hitler.

Bookseller: Well, he wasn't a film star, was he.

Customer: Yes, he was. He was American. Jewish, I think.

Bookseller: ...

Customer: I tell you something, you must get some odd requests, working here.

Customer: Hi, do you have any new books?

Bookseller: We're an antiquarian bookstore – our stock is made up of books which are out of print.

Customer: So other people have touched them?

Bookseller: ...Presumably, yes.

Customer: I don't think I'll bother, thanks.

Bookseller: ... Ok.

Customer: I have *The Pickwick Papers*, first edition. How much will you buy them for?

Bookseller *(examines book)*: Sorry, but this was was printed in 1910.

Customer: Yes.

Bookseller: *The Pickwick Papers* was first printed in 1837; this isn't a first edition.

Customer: No, it was definitely first printed in 1910.

Bookseller: Dickens was dead in 1910.

Customer: I don't think so. You're trying to con me.

Bookseller: I promise you, I'm not.

Customer: *(Glares for a while, then snatches the book back up)* I'm taking the book elsewhere! *(Storms out)*

Customer: Hi. We've just moved and we've found some really old books in the attic. Would you be interested in buying them?

Bookseller: That depends—what sort of books are they?

Customer: Well, one of them is a copy of *Gone with the Wind*, printed the in 1890s.

Bookseller: Well, you know, *Gone with the Wind* was written in the 1930s.

Customer: Well, yeah, but this is a really old copy.

Terry Dallas
Armchair Books, Pendleton, OR

◆

Customer: I'm looking for a signed copy of any book by Marcel Proust as a gift for my daughter.

Bookseller: I'm sorry, signed Proust material is very rare, but I can show you the books of his that we have in stock.

Customer *(after paying)*: Do you have a pen?

(Bookseller hands him a red pen. The customer opens the book to the title page and writes: "I hope you enjoy my book, Marcel Proust.")

◆

Customer: Do you have a copy of *Mrs. Dalloway*, but, like, really old—so from, like, 1850?

Bookseller: ...

◆

Customer: Some of these books are dusty. Can't you vacuum them?

Customer: Do you have any old copies of Dickens?
Bookseller: We've got a copy of *David Copperfield* from 1850 for $150.
Customer: Why is it so expensive if it's that old?

Customer: This book has a couple of tears to some of the pages.

Bookseller: Yes, unfortunately some of the older books haven't had as much love as they should have done from previous owners.

Customer: So, will you lower the price? It says here it's $20.

Bookseller: I'm sorry but we take into account the condition of the books when we price them; if that book was in a better condition, it would be worth a lot more than $20.

Customer: Well, you can't have taken this tear here into account *(points to page)* or this one here *(points to another page)*, because my son did those two minutes ago.

Bookseller: So, the book is now more damaged than it was before, because of your son?

Customer: Yes. Exactly. So will you lower the price?

◆

Customer: *(Drops an old, expensive book on the floor by accident)*: Great shot!

Bookseller: *(glares)*

Customer: I mean... sorry.

◆

Customer: Do you have a copy of Bella Swan's favorite book? You know, from *Twilight*? *(Bookseller sighs and pulls a copy of* Wuthering Heights *off the shelf)*

Customer: Do you have the one with the cover that looks like *Twilight*?

Bookseller: No. This is an antiquarian bookstore, so this is an old edition of the book.

Customer: But it's still the one with that girl Cathy and the dangerous guy, right?

Bookseller: Yes, it's still the story by Emily Brontë.

Customer: Right. Do you think they'll make it into a film?

Bookseller: They've made several films of it. The one where Ralph Fiennes plays Heathcliff is very good.

Customer: What? Voldemort plays Heathcliff?

Bookseller: Well...

Customer: But that's Edward's role.

Bookseller: *Wuthering Heights* was written well before both Harry Potter and *Twilight*.

Customer: Yeah, but Voldemort killed Cedric, who's played by Robert Pattinson, and now Voldemort's playing Edward's role in *Wuthering Heights*, because Edward's character is Heathcliff. I think that Emily Brontë's trying to say something about vampires.

Bookseller: … that's $10.

Customer: For what?

Bookseller: For the book.

Customer: Oh, no, it's ok, I'm going to go and try and find the Voldemort DVD version.

Bookseller: Right.

Customer: Thanks for all your help!

◆

(Phone rings)

Bookseller: Hello?

Customer: Hello, I've got some books I'd like to sell.

Bookseller: Sure. What kinds of books do you have?

Customer: Oh, boxes and boxes of stuff. I've got some children's books, some comics, some old magazines and newspapers, an exercise bike, a couple of art books and some cookbooks, too.

Bookseller: What was the one in the middle?

Customer: Erm. Old magazines.

Bookseller: No, the one after that.

Customer: An exercise bike.

Bookseller: Yes... we won't be wanting the exercise bike.

Bookseller: Hi, can I help?

Customer: Yes. I've got a copy of *The Secrets of Houdini* that I'd like to sell. It's very rare. And it's signed by Houdini himself.

Bookseller: Actually signed by Houdini?

Customer: Yes. *(hands book over)*

Bookseller: Ah *(upon noticing signature to frontispiece)*, I'm pretty sure that this signature is actually part of the printing.

Customer: Why?

Bookseller: Because the date next to the signature is 1924.

Customer: So?

Bookseller: Well, this book was printed in 1932.

Customer: Perhaps the date on the signature actually reads 1934.

Bookseller: In that case, the signature is fake.

Customer: Why?

Bookseller: Because Houdini died in 1926.

Customer: But if you feel the signature, you can tell that it's ridged. It doesn't feel like the rest of the page.

Bookseller: Yes, I see what you mean; it's almost like someone's gone over it with a pencil, isn't it?

Customer *(frowning)*: That is a genuine Houdini signature.

Bookseller: I assure you; it's part of the printing.

Customer: He signed the book himself.

Bookseller: And dated it 1924? In a book published in 1932? Six years after he died?

Customer: ... Perhaps it was his last unsolvable act of magic.

Bookseller: Unfortunately I don't think that Houdini's last cryptic trick was to come back from the dead, sign your book, and make you a whole lot of money.

Customer: ...

Customer: I've got some books I'd like to sell *(plonks them on the desk)*. I'd like twenty-five dollars for the lot.

Bookseller: Didn't you buy these from us last week?

Customer: Yes.

Bookseller: I see they've still got our prices in.

Customer: Uh-huh.

Bookseller: ... You didn't even pay twenty-five dollars for these in the first place.

Customer: Yes, but they're older now than they were last week, see. So they must be worth more.

Customer: I've got some books to sell.

Bookseller: Hi, thanks. I'm just helping some customers at the moment. Could you join the back of the line?

Customer: Er, I'm selling you books; I'm here for your benefit.

Bookseller: These other people are here to buy books, they are also here for the store's benefit.

Customer: You've got thirty seconds to buy them, or I'm leaving. You need to learn to prioritize.

◆

Customer: Do you have any second-hand crosswords?

Bookseller: You mean crosswords that have already been filled in?

Customer: Yes. I love crosswords, but they're ever so difficult.

◆

Customer *(holding up a copy of* Ulysses*)*: Why is this book so long? Isn't it supposed to be set in a single day? How can this many pages of things happen to one person in one day? I mean, I get up, have breakfast, go to work, come home... sometimes I might go out for a drink, and that's it! And, I mean, that doesn't fill a book, does it?

◆

Customer: Do you... um... pay, like, more for signed books?

Bookseller: For some books, yes, a signed copy would certainly be worth more.

Customer: What would you give me for... um... like, a signed copy of, like... *The Diary of Anne Frank*?

Bookseller: I would give you something like a
  billion dollars for that.

Customer: Oh, awesome!

Anonymous

Customer: Do you have Philip Pullman's *The Book
  of Dust*?

Bookseller: No, I don't think a publication date has
  even been set for that book yet.

Customer: I know, it's just I thought you might
  already have a copy, considering you're an
  antiquarian bookstore.

Bookseller: ... Antiquarian means old. We don't
  have books, you know, from the future.

Customer: Ah.

Customer: Do you have any old knitting patterns?

Bookseller: We do, as it happens, yes. They're
  over here.

Customer: And do you sell knitting needles?

Bookseller: No, I'm afraid not.

Customer: But I'll need those when using the old
  knitting patterns.

Bookseller: Well...

Customer: And do you sell wool?

Bookseller: No, just the knitting patterns and magazines.

Customer: You haven't thought this through properly, have you? How am I supposed to knit a scarf without knitting needles and wool?

Bookseller: You're going to have to buy those things from another store, I'm afraid.

Customer: It would be much better for me if I could buy everything in one place.

Bookseller: Unfortunately we can't stock everything relevant to the books we have, otherwise we'd be full of gardening tools, sewing machines, cooking ingredients and paint brushes.

Customer: What are you talking about? I don't need any of those things. I only need wool and knitting needles. I'm not going to knit with a paintbrush!

◆

Customer: I've always wondered how one writes a book.

Bookseller: How do you mean?

Customer: I mean, how did authors do it before computers were invented?

Bookseller: Well, there were typewriters and, before that, they wrote by hand.

Customer: You would have thought they could have invented computers faster to make writers' lives easier.

Bookseller: ... Yes.

Customer: And then, now that they have computers, is there a program that they use?

Bookseller: A program?

Customer: A computer program that you know, puts everything in the right order. Tells you what to name your characters and things.

Bookseller: No, I don't think so. Well, I'm sure that there are programs with guidelines but I don't think people tend to use them. They just write.

Customer: They just write?

Bookseller: Yes, they just write the story they want to tell.

Customer: So they just use something like Word?

Bookseller: Yes, I guess so.

Customer: But, you see, that's what I really don't understand.

Bookseller: What?

Customer: Well Word documents are 8½ x 11 and a book is never that big. It's a lot smaller.

Bookseller: ...

Customer: So, how on earth do they get it all to fit?

Bookseller: ...

WEIRD THINGS CUSTOMERS SAY AT *WEIRD THINGS CUSTOMERS SAY IN BOOKSTORES* BOOK SIGNINGS

Standing in a bookstore with copies of *Weird Things* to sign was bound to get a few strange looks, and perhaps confuse a couple of people, but I think I underestimated the irony of me going into a bookstore, with *Weird Things Customers Say in Bookstores,* and interacting with the customers . . .

—author Jen Campbell

◆

Man: *Weird Things Customers Say in Bookstores* by Jen Campbell?

Me: Yep.

Man: You wrote this?

Me: I did.

Man: Cool. What's your name?

Me: . . . Jen Campbell.

Man *(seriously)*: And what's the book about? Is it a thriller or something? Does it have vampires? I love vampires.

Woman: Can you tell me where the children's section is?

Me: I'm afraid I don't work here—I'm just here signing books today.

Woman: Oh. Well, what use is that?!

◆

Customer: All writers are millionaires, aren't they?

Me: Nope.

Customer: How much do you earn, then?

◆

Customer: I recognize you. Were you on television?

Me: Nope, not that I'm aware of.

Customer: You were! I've seen you.

Me: I don't think so. I'm a writer.

Customer: Oh. Wait. Are there secret cameras here? Is this a fly-on-the-wall documentary?

Me: . . . No. I'm, er, just signing books.

Customer: Well, you would say that, wouldn't you? Hmmm. Wait a minute, I'm just going to nip to the bathroom and do my makeup. Then I'll come back and we can have this conversation again.

◆

Man: *Weird Things*, eh?

Me: Yep.

Man: You should follow my wife around; she says
stupid things all the time.

Me: Really?

Man: Yeah. Not necessarily in bookstores, just in life.

Me: Oh.

Man: Yeah. Like, she tells people that I poisoned
our cat. But I totally didn't.

◆

Woman *(walks up to me, holding up a copy of* Fifty
Shades of Grey*)*: Will you sign this for me?

Me: . . . I didn't write that book.

Woman: But the sign here says that you're signing
books today.

Me: Yes . . . I'm signing the book that I wrote (*indicates* Weird Things)

Woman: Just that one?

Me: . . . Yes.

Woman: Not any of the others?

Me: . . . No.

Woman: Oh, well, that's very odd. *(She wanders off,
looking confused.)*

Woman: So. Are you the new J. K. Rowling, then? You don't look like her. You've got different hair.

I HAVE AN IDEA FOR A BOOK

Customer: I'd love to write a book.

Bookseller: Then you should write one.

Customer: I really don't have the time.

Bookseller: I'm sure you could make time.

Customer: No, you don't get it; I really don't have the time. I had my fortune read on Monday, and the fortuneteller lady said that I'm going to get knocked down by a bus next week. She said that it'll probably kill me.

Bookseller: . . . Oh. Well, er, that doesn't sound very nice.

Customer: No, it doesn't, does it? It's really annoying, too, 'cause I'd booked a vacation for next month, and I was really looking forward to it.

Customer: I'd like a book for a friend about saving the world from alien invasion. I'd like the main character to be a little like Freddie Mercury and a little like Arnold Schwarzenegger. Does anything spring to mind?

◆

Customer: I don't like poetry. It seems so arbitrary. *(Pause)* Wait, that rhymes! Perhaps I'm an undiscovered poet.

Bookseller: I thought you didn't like poetry?

Customer: Well, not other people's—but I would probably like my own!

◆

Customer: I'm looking for books for an eight-year-old girl. What would you recommend?

Bookseller: Well, is she a confident reader for her age?

Customer: Yes.

Bookseller: And what are her interests?

Customer: Horses, princesses, dancing . . .

Bookseller: OK—I'll help you find some.

(Bookseller spends the next ten minutes finding books for the customer, talking about each one in turn.)

Customer: Great. Thanks. I'll bear all those in mind.

Bookseller: Would you like us to keep any on reserve for you?

Customer *(gets out pen and paper to write down the titles)*: No, I'll just write them down. I don't want them myself. I'm writing a book, you see, about an eight-year-old girl and I wanted to work out what books she should have on her bookcase.

Bookseller: So you don't want to buy any?

Customer: Oh, no dear. Don't be silly. I might have the character purchase some of the books in the story itself. But not in real life.

Bookseller: . . . I see.

Customer: And, to be honest, my character's rather advanced for her age with regard to technology. So I might have her buy them online instead.

Bookseller: . . . Right.

◆

Customer: There are several things I look for in a good book.

Bookseller: Oh? What are those?

Customer: A murder—preferably of a handsome young man—a helicopter ride, a small dog, a parrot, a suicide, cigars, moustaches, love letters and animals that have escaped from the zoo.

Bookseller: . . .

Customer: Why aren't you writing these things down?

Bookseller: Sorry *(grabs a pen)*.

Customer: Good. Let's not forget the mysterious crop circles in the fields. Then there's the heroine—preferably a redhead from a country house in Wales, who collects fossils in her spare time. Her grandmother should be alive, but only just, and on the weekends she should ride wild horses on the beach. The heroine, that is, not the grandmother.

Bookseller: . . . Right.

Customer: Any books spring to mind?

Bookseller: No . . . It sounds like you should probably write this book yourself, considering you have such specific tastes.

Customer: You know, I rather hoped you might say that. *(He pulls a notebook out of his pocket.)* I've been outlining the story. Would you like to read it?

IMAGINARY FRIENDS

Child *(to bookseller)*: Does Santa come to your bookstore to get gifts for kids?

Bookseller *(nodding wisely)*: Yes. Yes. He does.

Child: That's awesome!

Bookseller: Yes, it is.

Child: But . . .

Bookseller: But what?

Child: But . . . Santa's really fat. I don't think he could squeeze down the corridors between the bookshelves.

Bookseller: It's OK. He sends us a list beforehand, and we leave the books by the door.

Child *(impressed)*: That makes you Santa's elf!

Bookseller: Yes . . . yes, I suppose it does.

Young Boy: When I grow up, I'm going to be a book ninja.

Bookseller: Cool! What do book ninjas do?

Young Boy: I can't tell you. It's top secret.

Little Boy: Do you have any superpowers?

Bookseller: Sadly, I don't think I do. Do you?

Little Boy *(whispers)*: Yes. I can fly. But only when no one else is watching

Customer: I need to return this book *(produces* The Iron Man *by Ted Hughes)*.

Bookseller: Is there a problem?

Customer: Yes! It doesn't have Robert Downey Jr. in it. AT ALL.

Customer: Are you prepared?

Bookseller: . . . For what?

Customer: For the zombie apocalypse.

Young Girl *(pointing to a cupboard under one of the bookshelves)*: Can you get to Narnia through there?

Bookseller: Unfortunately, I don't think you can.

Young Girl: Oh. Our wardrobe at home doesn't work for getting to Narnia, either.

Bookseller: No?

Young Girl: No. Dad says it's because Mom bought it at IKEA.

(Bookseller sees a customer putting some garlic on a bookshelf)

Bookseller: . . . Er, excuse me, can I ask what you're doing?

Customer: These books are about vampires. I'm taking precautions.

Little Boy *(whispers)*: You should stock up on food.
Bookseller: Should I?
Little Boy: Yes.
Bookseller: Why?
Little Boy *(seriously)*: The aliens are coming.
Bookseller: . . . They are?
Little Boy: Yes. ET is angry, and he wants revenge!

Customer: Where are your books on war?
Bookseller: They'll be in with history. Our history section is split up into British History, European History, American History and World History. Which war are you looking for, specifically?
Customer: I want a history of the ongoing war between werewolves and vampires.
Bookseller: . . .
Customer: Where would I find that?

Customer: I need to return this book on ghosts.
Bookseller: Is there a problem with it?
Customer: Yes. It's haunted.

Susan Holland: SmithBooks,
Victoria, British Columbia, Canada.

ACKNOWLEDGMENTS

Oodles of thanks to my wonderful agent, Charlie Campbell, who used to be a bookseller in Paris. He once served a customer who spat cheese soufflé all over him. He still doesn't know why they did that.

Many thanks to my lovely UK editor, Hugh Barker, who used to work at Ripping Yarns.

Big love to Greg for the wonderful illustrations, especially for the crucified bunny rabbit.

Many thanks to the lovely people of Constable and Robinson, The Overlook Press, and Ed Victor.

Thanks and love to Vanessa, Malcolm, Becky, Polly [and Magnus], and to Celia, Sasha, Sherry, Marie, Gloria, Lucinda and Zoe.

Thank you to the booksellers who submitted their own "Weird Things." It was heart-warming [and hilarious] to confirm that customers are saying strange things in bookstores worldwide.

Many thanks to Neil Gaiman and all the wonderful people of Twitter who enjoyed, and spread the word about, "Weird Things."

Thanks and love to my wonderful friends and family.

Thank you Miles.